For Gran,
Margaret Craig
McDougall

Illustrations copyright © 1994 by Louise Voce

First U.S. edition 1994
Published in Great Britain in 1994 by Walker Books Ltd., London.

Library of Congress Cataloging-in-Publication Data
Voce, Louise.
Over in the meadow : a traditional counting rhyme / Louise Voce.—1st U.S. ed.

"Published in Great Britain in 1994 by Walker Books Ltd., London"—T.p.verso.
Summary: A traditional counting rhyme describing the activities of various
baby animals, from one turtle to ten foxes.
ISBN 1-56402-428-8
[1. Animals—Infancy—Fiction. 2. Counting. 3. Stories in rhyme.] I. Title.
PZ8.3.V82Ov 1994
[E]—dc20   93-21294

2 4 6 8 10 9 7 5 3 1

Printed in Italy

The pictures in this book were done in watercolor inks.

Candlewick Press
2067 Massachusetts Avenue
Cambridge, Massachusetts 02140

OVER IN THE MEADOW

A Traditional Counting Rhyme

Louise Voce

CANDLEWICK PRESS

CAMBRIDGE, MASSACHUSETTS

Over in the meadow
in the sand in the sun . . .

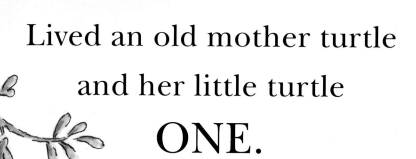

Lived an old mother turtle
and her little turtle
ONE.

"Dig," said his mother.
"I dig," said the One.
So he dug all day
in the sand in the sun.

Over in the meadow
where the stream runs blue,
Lived an old mother duck
and her little ducklings
TWO.
"Quack," said their mother.
"We quack," said the Two.
So they quacked all day
where the stream runs blue.

Over in the meadow
in a hole in a tree,
Lived an old mother owl
and her little owls
THREE.
"Who-whoo," said their mother.
"Who-whoo," said the Three.
So they who-whooed all day
in a hole in a tree.

Over in the meadow
by the big barn door,
Lived an old mother mouse
and her little mice
FOUR.
"Squeak," said their mother.
"We squeak," said the Four.
So they squeaked all day
by the big barn door.

Over in the meadow
in a snug beehive,
Lived an old mother bee
and her little bees
FIVE.
"Buzz," said their mother.
"We buzz," said the Five.
So they buzzed all day
round their snug beehive.

Over in the meadow
in a nest built of sticks,
Lived an old mother squirrel
and her little squirrels
SIX.
"Jump," said their mother.
"We jump," said the Six.
So they jumped all day
round their nest built of sticks.

Over in the meadow
where the grass grows so even,
Lived an old mother frog
and her little froggies
SEVEN.
"Hop!" said their mother.
"We hop!" said the Seven.
So they hopped all the day
where the grass grows so even.

Over in the meadow
near the little mossy gate,
Lived an old mother lizard
and her little lizards
EIGHT.
"Run," said their mother.
"We run," said the Eight.
So they ran all day
on the little mossy gate.

Over in the meadow
by the tall green pine,
Lived an old mother pig
and her little piglets
NINE.
"Oink!" said their mother.
"We oink," said the Nine.
So they oinked all day
near the tall green pine.

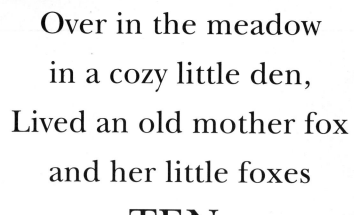

Over in the meadow
in a cozy little den,
Lived an old mother fox
and her little foxes
TEN.
"Play," said their mother.
"We play," said the Ten.
So they played all day
round their cozy little den.

Over in the meadow
in the sand in the sun . . .

1  digs

2  quack

3  who-whoo

4  squeak

5  buzz

6 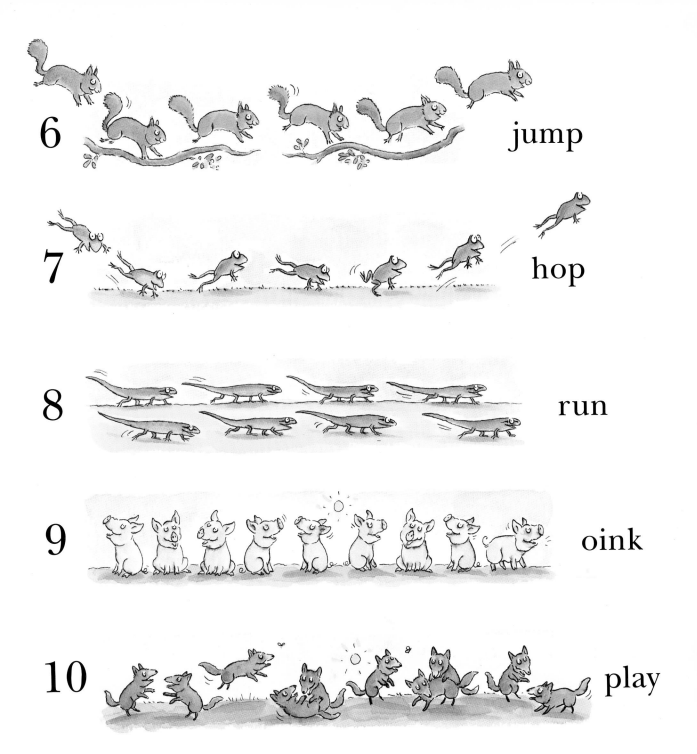 jump

7 hop

8 run

9 oink

10 play

over in the meadow till the end of the day.